Sound Sleeping
in
the neighborhood
™

Sound Sleeping in the neighborhood T.M.

by Jerry Van Amerongen

Andrews and McMeel
A Universal Press Syndicate Company
Kansas City • New York

ISBN: 0-8362-1802-7

Library of Congress Catalog Card Number: 87-73260

───────────── ATTENTION: SCHOOLS AND BUSINESSES ─────────────

Brad's not much of a reader.

PRINCIPLE OF MODERN DIPLOMACY: There's nothing like a little face-to-face chat to clear away misunderstandings and paranoia.

Since joining Diet Watchers Anonymous, Noel Cramer continues to be surprised at just how comprehensive the group's services are.

Glenn's code of behavior doesn't permit him to be seen in his bathrobe.

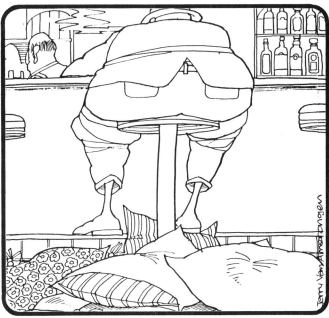

Now this is what you call your serious drinker.

The Hemelshots like to keep tabs on their dog Lionel.

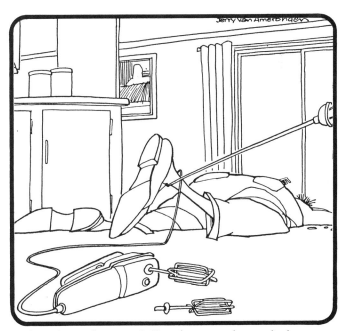

Another of materialism's countless victims

Ted needs 10 to 15 minutes of private, unreachable inner space per day, no matter what.

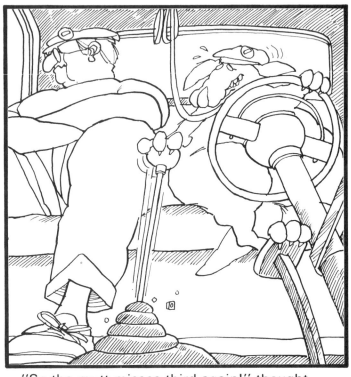

"So the mutt misses third again!" thought Carl with smoldering disdain.

Allen sizes up another challenger prior to the men's finals of the Tall Hair Contest.

Jason's dream of a sophisticated evening fades as his date proudly shows off her new chair with the western motif.

Ironically, the extension agent was just saying there seemed to be no visible explanation for such a groove.

Albert's feet were too big for the bird suit.

"It's my fault, Officer. The dog should never have been driving!"

"Edwin, try not to catch his eye. . . ."

Elmer Erdman is a man who slips out after midnight to break simple traffic laws.

You can always tell when Uncle Lyle gets tired of horsing around with the dog.

Ranching as a labor-intensive business

After long years of study, Dr. Bing was disheartened to find the speech patterns of the common rat consisted primarily of expletives aimed directly at him.

Used-car manager Monte Sly makes the subtle transition from entrepreneur to professional.

"What a relief," thought Pernell.

Biff noticed the cat just as it disappeared down the laundry chute.

Although the opportunity to work with troubled, smaller dogs is endless, pet therapist Angela Simms is going to restrict her practice to larger dogs.

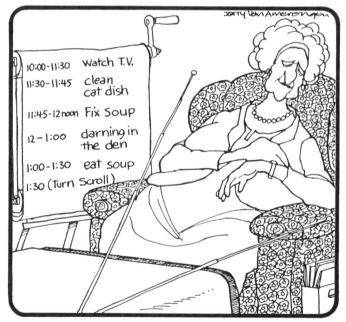

Brenda's strict regimen offers a refuge from confusion.

Judy readies herself for a big sale.

To say only that Sheldon enjoys electronics is to avoid a deeper issue.

Outside at the Indigestion Institute

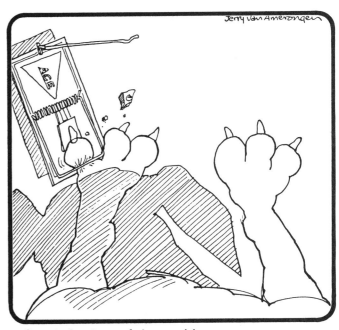

Sparky's view of the problem

Too bad for Murphy and Scooter. Their master has succumbed to the trendy idea of carrying hand weights while jogging.

It doesn't pay to get a late start on Saturday morning.

Georgio Menucci, the clown prince of pasta

"That's it for motorized socks!" thought Lyle.

It sounded like a loud, vaguely familiar dog who barked twice and then hung up.

A quiet moment with the man who founded the college that trains TV news directors.

A gathering of active listeners

Steve is confronted with strong evidence that he has been keeping a chicken during office hours.

Believing anxiety to be a positive life force, Brad prepares for another day.

Once again Mrs. Coupner chills Arnold's ice cream beyond the manufacturer's recommendation.

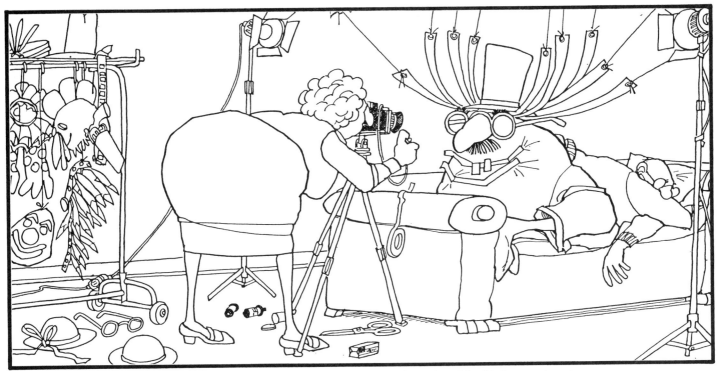

It's easy to see why Mrs. Habner never hassles Mr. Habner about being a sound sleeper.

"Ladies, it's Saturday night. Do you know where your Naval Vet is? . . ."

As an animal deprogrammer, Carl Simpe was accustomed to this sort of abuse.

Brad half expected a memo like this. It reads, "Please, no sheepskins during business hours."

Shawn remains bedeviled by mechanical ineptitude.

Snake-lover Arnold Striker is beginning to love dogs even more.

Vacation notes: Another tourist with something to tell the neighbors

Willard set the idle much too high.

Thomas yearns to know a stable woman.

Edwin loses bodily functions during quiet times.

Knowing her ill-tempered husband lashes out at inanimate objects only, Phyllis keeps on the move.

An encounter group for owners of unsightly pets

How ironic! At this very moment, in another community, Mrs. Herber is saying to Mr. Herber, "Heaven only knows what our son, Vernon, is up to right now."

TRIVIA TOUGHIE: Who played Lassie?

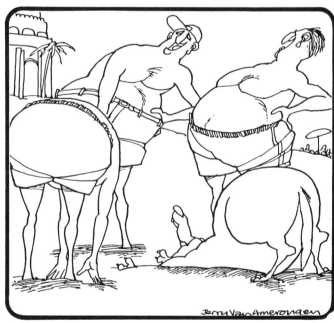

Vacation notes: A friendly, informal discussion about back problems

Profiles in Bad Luck: Herb Stanley sits
in front of a barber whose business
recently failed.

THE SINGING PSYCHIATRIST

David has next to no luck playing the
game, "Reach the can before the other
cans come."

Marcus kills two birds with one stone.

A man with an irrational fear of falling

Portrait of a man with too much time on his hands.

So much for that annoying little beeping sound of Allen's alarm watch.

Adrian celebrates telecommunications week.

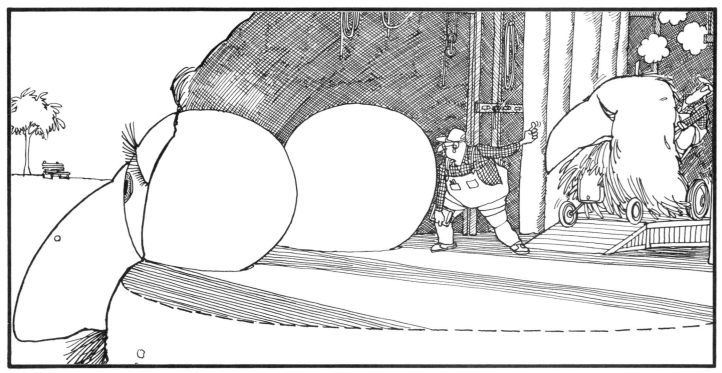

A man about to experience a fleeting image

Chicken farmer Dwight Bangsaddle toys with the idea of starting a duck pond.

Actually, neither shampoo "A" nor shampoo "B" seemed right for Nathan.

"Why is Dr. Reims going on and on about green, leafy vegetables?" wondered Tom.

It's Sunday afternoon, and Mrs. Harkney is lashing out at fast-food restaurants again.

It's Aaron's job to identify and tranquilize jive roller-skaters.

It may be over between Nathan and Sylvia, but it's not over between Nathan and the dog, Bruno.

The electrified bug suit . . . perfect for those quiet summer evenings

Where you find Eddie Bowhusker you find his pet mice, Shawn and Andrea.

Martin still isn't "one with his horse."

Norman takes walking very seriously.

Another tourist snuffed by a poorly maintained monument

Wanting his subjects to share in the excitement, wildlife photographer Barnie Flowers uses only the self-developing kind of film.

It burns Mrs. Herns up when Phillip putters around the house.

Bernard searches out narrow staircases.

Brad continues to challenge his bodily functions by changing his access routes to the butter.

For footstool artisan Murry Hemmings, art mirrors life.

Mrs. Harvey's afternoon is punctuated by drama.

Life is difficult for the organizationally impaired.

Cynthia's mind is like a sparkler.

For Mrs. Herns, life is about to take a dark turn. Mr. Herns has just seized upon the concept of a circular saw as a musical instrument.

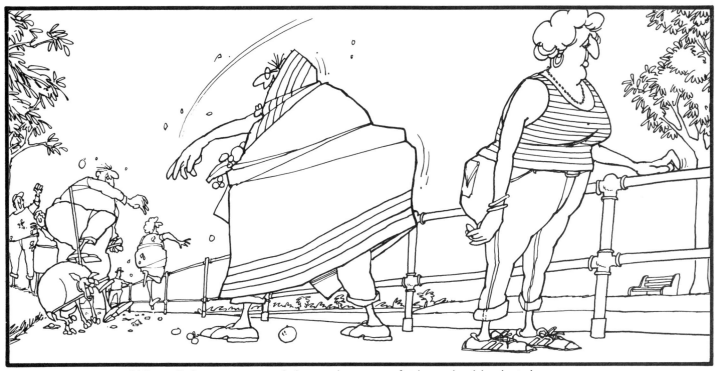

When Brian suggested they take some fruit and a blanket down to the lake, Shirley had hoped his intentions were more romantic in nature.

Without thinking, Sylvan waves hello to his personal banker and goodbye to his personal loan application.

Gerald mistook the sound of a 10-horse-power Evinrude for a tear in his double-knits.

Mrs. Gelpie is just glad they've never had any really major electrical problem.

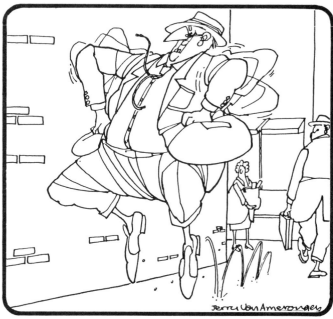

Jason is walking one of the narrower planks in the great boardwalk of life.

Tom slips into his long pants.

Mr. Shimmers worries about becoming an "A" personality.

Little Audrey's gotten a lot more help and understanding since she pointed her father out to her teacher.

Spirits sag among the competitors as Norm's raccoon continues with a flawless recital of Verdi's *Rigoletto*.

Arnold's pet worm means another night in the back seat of the Mercury.

Once again Gloria finds herself denying the reality of another evening at home.

No wonder you forever hear Mrs. Nearsby's vacuum going.

The stranger drew a suspicious glance from proprietor Kirby as he made his way toward the model kits.

Francine is the kind of person who gives
city slickers a bad name.

Anthony leads a dog's life.

This is one of Harold's Tours' least
expensive packages.

Sherman really loves his eaves.

"Be real careful with Mr. Arnham's car, Smitty, he's got his spiritual adviser with him today."

Fred Thurston displays another aspect of his chameleon-like personality.

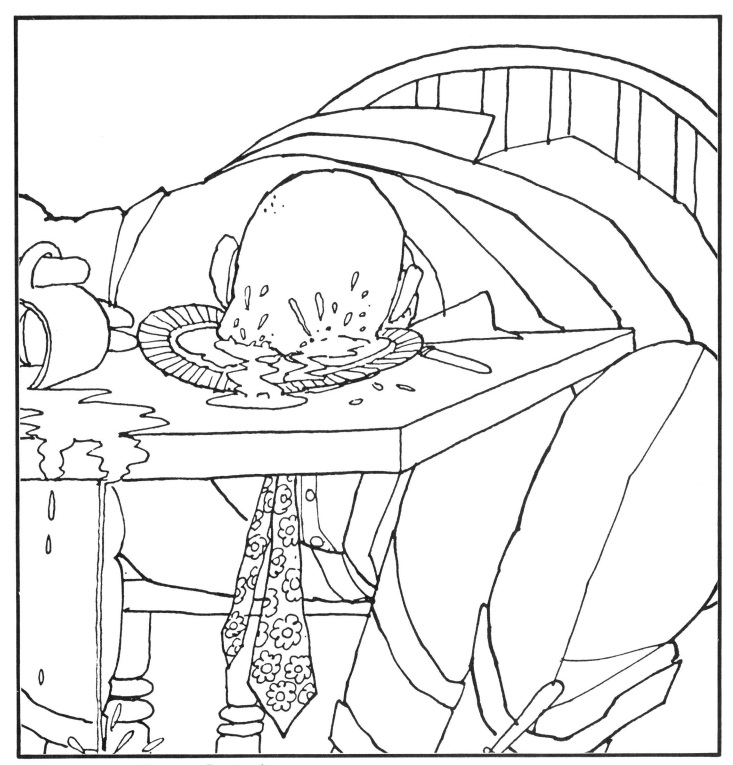

Eggs put Ben to sleep.

Fowler is a first-semester freshman.

With outside help, Newton makes the transition from wing tip to sport casual.

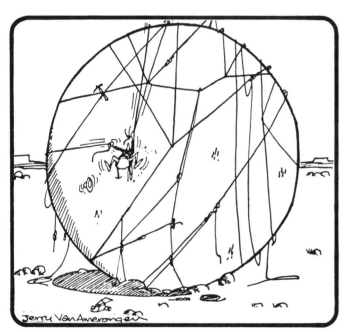

Marble rock proves to be a tough climb.

Someone or something was pulling Skipper's nose from inside.

"What does it mean," worried Allen. "This sudden outbreak of sweaty feet?"

Norman Feidler works for a local dairy.

Alex stalls for time until he can remember why he wandered into the hardware department.

Another affront to the English language

Profiles in bad luck: Norton Sears discovers the man upstairs has organized a weekly polka fest.

Nature's unrelenting presence

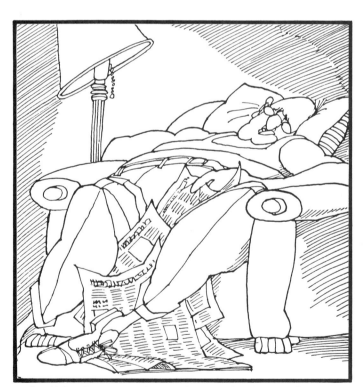

Cyril isn't so much waxing as he is waning.

With 11 years in the recliner business, Bob has all but forgotten his dream of being a test pilot.

They say you can tell the cut of a man's jib by the way he handles himself around the slips . . . Carl Shothammer is pretty much jibless.

Ernest lounges over his third cheese and onion enchilada.

Sinus treatment: The early years

Arthur's no longer the "sturdy oak" of the family.

With a little sigh of hope, Sparky leans closer to Clarence.

Dr. Samuels didn't mince words: "You believe you're a small red fox, and you require treatment."

Even with the new flippers, Edmond appears unable to master the fundamentals of a strong forward stroke.

This is pretty much how the evenings go after Shawn has spicy food for supper.

Lawrence remains painfully awkward as a public speaker.

Simple pleasure

Vinnie is a half-hearted meddler.

Albert's life, once a frothing white water, has dwindled to an intermittent bottomland seepage.

Halfway through his "Hearty Man" breakfast, Dwayne thought he heard some of his smaller arteries slamming shut.

"You were sitting off-center again, weren't you, Spencer?"

Martin puts a stop to "Cherry Pink and Apple Blossom White."

Millie looked up just in time to notice that the brunch, being prepared on the balcony above, would be one egg short.

Raymond shows us his new doghouse made entirely of used breakfast trays.

New ideas rush into Allen's mind pell-mell, crowding old ones out before they take form or shape.

Frequent-flyer Bruce Rancors interacts with a fellow traveler who cranked his seat all the way back.

Madam Wonderstar told Bob he was gonna catch a cold . . . and that's all she told him.

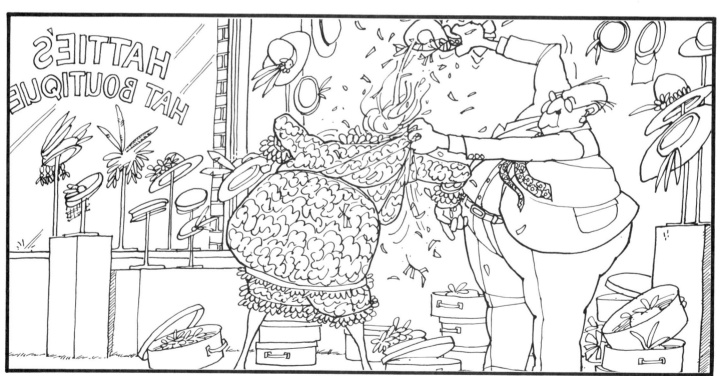

Mr. Seemy's temperament doesn't fit the personality of the shop.

Jonathan finishes the paper on the porch as Elizabeth and "Smurfy Murphy" sit down to read.

Future archaeologists unearth yet another relic from the "age of vanity."

Samuel discovers he has a skill deficiency.

As soon as convict Hargrove realized the cell was designed to resemble an automotive service lounge, he began to struggle.

Mindful of the stress factor and its effect on cholesterol build-up, Jason begins to monitor easy-to-get-at arteries.

A sense of uneasiness moved through the crowd.

Mr. Narby is a slave to those with balanced, orderly minds.

Smitty over in meats feels he's identified another vegetarian.

Boyd demands to see the Water's Edge Resort brochure again.

Allen suddenly wondered if his pores were open.

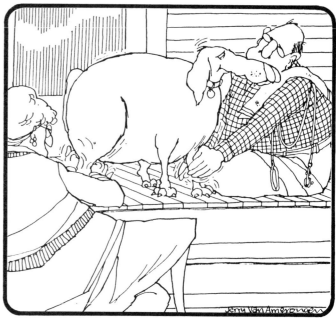

A brisk ankle rub keeps Skipper from cramping up during his morning walk.

A real mean dog enters his house.

Probably some sort of secret society

Mr. Murphy helps his wife wrap a present.

"Shouldn't you take the flashlight, Sylvan? It's already mid-afternoon."

Lightbulb tester Arnie Slocum fidgets in his sleep.

"Now you've got me doing it!"

It was testimony to Artie's optimistic nature that he didn't take the new regulations personally.

Evidently Morris figured out how to get the batteries into the control unit.

Cohabitation Axiom No. 6: The less it appears you know how to do, the less you'll have to do.

You actually have to have an appointment to see
Mrs. Sardyke's laundry.

Mrs. Nimmer serves notice . . . no
more horseplay!

Mechanic/Psychologist Murry Singer in session with a motorist prior to another round of repairs.

Darrell is a no-nonsense dreamer.

Mrs. Gelpie's creations are unsightly but delicious.

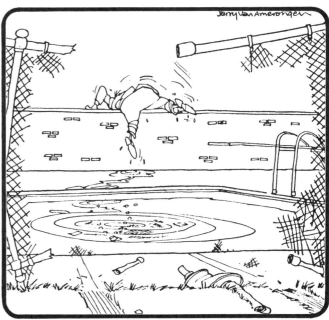

After a night of revelry Jason locates a nearby pool.

At times, life fits Emily like a cheap suit.

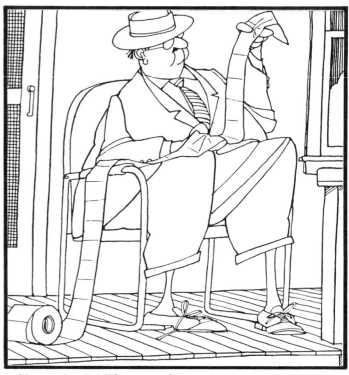

Not only did life pass Aaron by, it never even gave him a sideways glance.

Spot was struck by the beauty and power of Bennett's perfect voice expression.

A formerly married man of indifferent status

The Spiveys are thinking about going off their vegetarian diet.

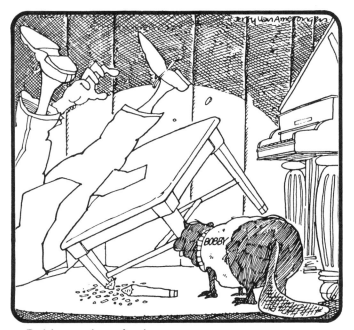

Bobby makes Andre mess up.

Do we really know what goes on in our department stores?

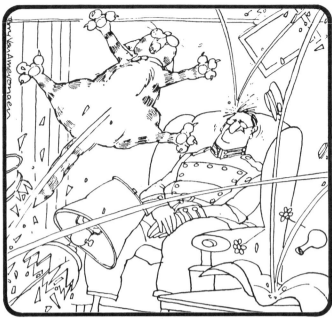

At home with Professor Darnell and Rosco, the acrobatic cat.

"Lizard party, your table's ready."

Freddy Fernhocker shows us his Tinker Toy Tongue Hanger.

The Bashskys wished their neighbor was more of a loner.

The evening was a delightful success. Rita had a charming wit, and Randolph was droll and amusing.

Another tourist who wishes he hadn't stubbornly attempted to use the "native tongue" to make his hotel accommodations.

Edwin carries a full set of silverware at all times.

Nature's law: The birdie who catches the most fishies gets to stand on any beak he wants to for a day.

Bernard is struck by the principles of aerodynamics.

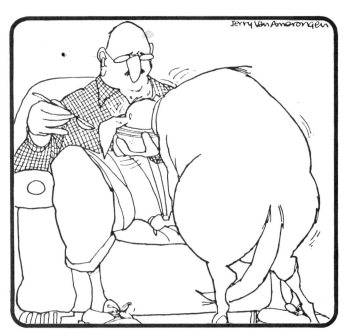

Interest in Carl's oatmeal is now unanimous.

Bob plays simple melodies on his teeth when he eats. (Generally, he eats alone.)

Adrian is no freshman in the college of love.

Edgar has no real sense of community.

Tired of waiting on hold all the time, Jason trained his dog to bark when he hears the wimpy, background music stop.

Bob Stemrack skitters around the linoleum, on simulated cat paws, five minutes every day.

Biffy's response to Spike's challenge is immediate.

Some pets bond to people more strongly than others.

Little did Cynthia realize that Aaron's taste in shirts was only one link in a strangely tragic chain.

Rather than shrink from her husband's crude remarks, Angela makes a positive coping gesture.

Sensing the madam's interest in "feathered adulation," Spencer makes a shrewd choice.

Bob has lost the sequence of his thoughts.

Gerald notices the container has one of those new "easy-off caps."

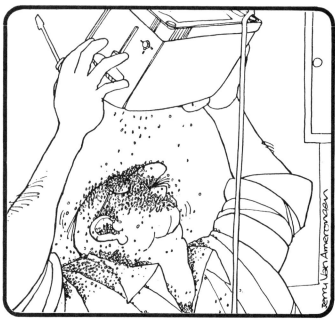

Paul's candle of household knowledge has burnt to a sorry stub.

Introducing the winner of the Mrs. Beautiful Tooth Contest.

Make no mistake; Ben has harmed his share of records.

Doing the Wave over at the Hemelshots

After 20 years of trying to keep up with Mrs. Herber's sprightly
walking manner, Mr. Herber's got a couple of bad knees.

Phillip makes road noises with his mouth when he drives.

Nobody's taking Bob Farney's candidacy seriously.

Sylvan's snide comment went something like this, "You don't see any ashtrays, do you lady?"

Ron lets a negative feeling out.

After some perusal, Jason decides to stay home.

Body Fat Analyst Sherman Sains' mind soon drifts back to work.

Alison's struggles with depth perception continue.

Tiny Arbuckle gets his share of parking tickets.

The next contestant is going to impersonate North Dakota.

Would this weekend be like all the other weekends with Bernard?
Elizabeth wondered.

Vanessa is smug because she has high arches.

How our ego is affected when the message is guilt.

Shortly thereafter, costume designer
Murray Stipples moved back to the city.

Mrs. Herns wondered if there might not be
some kind of adjustment that controlled the
amount of suction.

Tom remains skeptical of any slight
pleasure that might come his way.

Earl is stunningly protective of his wife.

Carl's cardboard glider is a disappointment.

"I sense you're a man of profound ideals."

The McGerkeys—not the sort of folks you'd want to have living upstairs

Adrian's house sits on a little-known mink migratory route.

Every morning Paul takes Biffy out to bark at the pigeons.

Elizabeth actually is fooling her body into thinking it feels good.

Ben pauses to tidy up a little shrine he's recently put together for himself.

There appears to be a pause in Gloria's search for organizational excellence.

Bob interfaces with Allen.

A man with too many male hormones

Berle is dangerous with power tools.

Conroy possesses a mocking spirit.

One small but ominous hand gesture
from Mrs. Gurkey and Mr. Gurkey quiets
right down.

Sandra and Jim do silly little relay races in their living room.

A meeting of two men in Velcro suits

Shawn looks over the manuscript of his new book titled *My Life With Tea*.

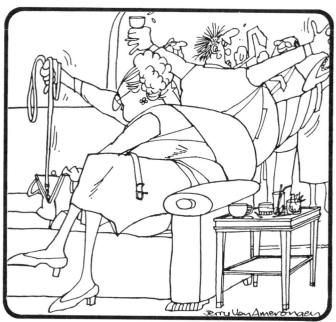

Mr. Farney doesn't know it yet, but he's going home.

One of the real estate agent's clients locates a structural defect.

Aaron locates one of the lodge's elusive bullfrogs.

"Release the fly!"

Interestingly enough the dog was named
Civil Disobedience.

Genevieve is proud of her humility.

Phyllis goes from person to personality.

Jason was drawn to men's cosmetics
because of their manly packaging concepts.

Mr. Harkey's chair is acting up again.

The Phillips brothers are about to be proven wrong.

Ben's never been in a restaurant where he hasn't found an empty hanger.

When the brain dredges something up from the darkest recesses of our psyche

Professional petter Noel Bannester prepares for work.

Ben brings out the best in Cynthia's pleaser personality.

Walking the minnow proves tedious for Samuel.

Then, just when Thomas thought the horseflies actually saw him as someone to fear. . .

Cheese is bad for Richard.

Because she picks up other people's energy, Marjorie becomes confused around crowds.

Lulled by the hum of human voices, calmed by the darkness,
and dulled by quantities of tiny chocolate candies, Elliot slips
into slumber.

The car's heat-sensing controls are activated by a little punk named
Eddie ''Body Heat'' Scruggins.

Nathan remains contrary to his upbringing.

Allen writes the National Coffee Institute to see if anything can be done.

Eric's adult interests have nearly put a stop to his adult charisma.

So it begins, thought new car owner Thomas Airington.

The incline was steeper than Bob thought.

As the day wore on, there were those among us who looked for someone to blame.

If you saw how he whipped them up, you wouldn't eat Byron's scrambled eggs either.

SHOULD I, OR SHOULDN'T I?...

OVERCOMING INDECISION

Ronald loses his place.

Jason's off the program.

Tom's idea of a big night is to stick around the house
and down a couple of Del Monte pear halves.

A real slouch of a flower enthusiast

Doberman in a conciliatory mood

Psychologist J.R. Reimes feels a sense of relief as work begins on his latest book, *Attraction to Lighting Is Normal and Healthy*.

Thanks to a natural draft between the buildings, Mr. Harkey almost never pays attention to local paper drives.

This is the photo that pretty much cost Sen. Airington his reelection bid.

This makes three times Wilson forgot about the Tinkertoys.

Suddenly Sparky's instinctive feelings become muddled with his trained feelings.

They delivered the wrong statue to the Metropolitan Men's Club.

There are people with elevated self-images, and then there's Jason Hamilton Biggs.

Bill Spettle spends his weekends enjoying over seven hours of videotape he's pieced together from various marine amusement parks.

Ben listens to his feelings.

Weren't you getting pretty sick of hearing about golf-ball-sized hail?!

The annual meeting of the National Society of Metal Detectors

"People don't laugh enough." That's the idea behind Bernard's mask-making.

Observing the anniversary of wood — a very old celebration

Louis was ashamed to be reminded of how he once ate.

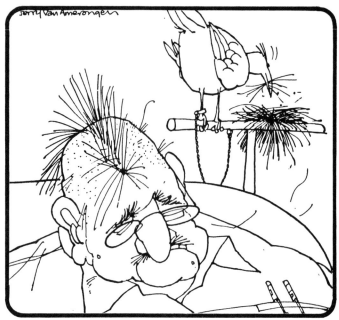

An aggressive pet with a nesting instinct, and an unusually boring book, conspire to give Edwin a punkish look.

All in all, it was the worst pile of mail Ben could remember receiving.

Shirley LaRoy likes to read poetry while being accompanied by her husband on chimes.

Mr. Harkey's interest in large, heavily weighted shoes is tugging away at the spontaneity of his marriage.

Brad encounters another really tough crossword puzzle.

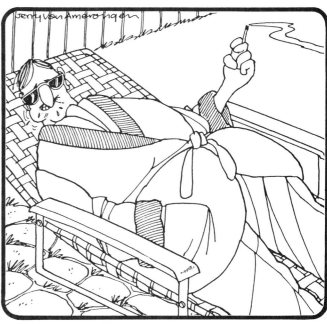

Voice talent Nathan Dobbs does cricket impersonations for nature films and some cowboy movies.

Mrs. Higgs knew her husband better than anyone.

Bernard's not ready for New Age music.

It pleases Carl to know he's guessed, within one-eighth of an inch, the width of another inanimate object.

Bob continues to differ with Mrs. Chambers concerning the taste of "really good" coffee.

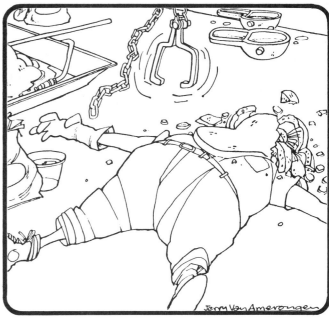

Shaken by his encounter with the cats, it would be several minutes before Allen discovered the rubber mouse taped to his forehead.

Gordon's initial test proves there's precious little future for concrete caps.

By enunciating forcefully with her mouth closed, Elizabeth can speak through her cheeks.

A virtual outsider disturbs Bob's spiritual tranquility.

The relatives keep an eye on Uncle Morrie, who seems to enjoy slipping away from family gatherings to steal cold cuts.

Ben's becoming more and more of a doer.

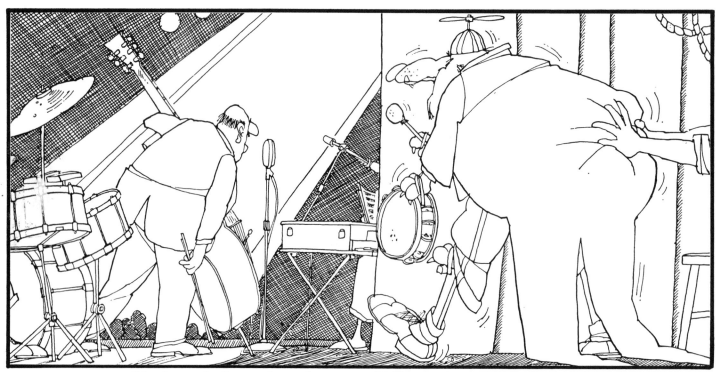

"And now ladies and gentlemen, we'd like to change the pace. . . ."

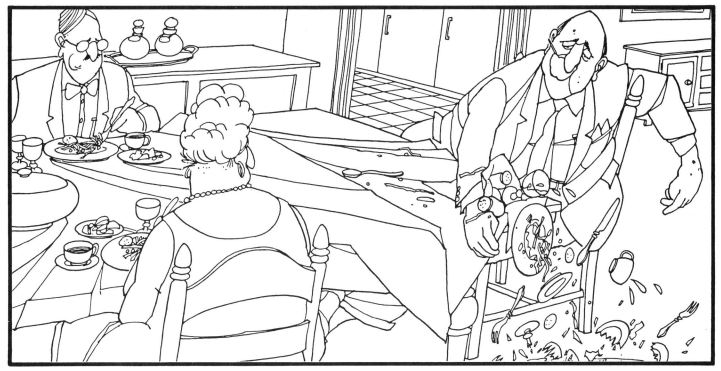

Uncle Harvey appears to be finished.

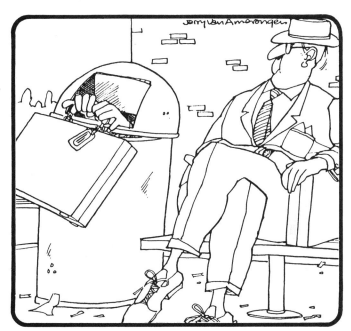

Lawrence remains ill at ease in public.

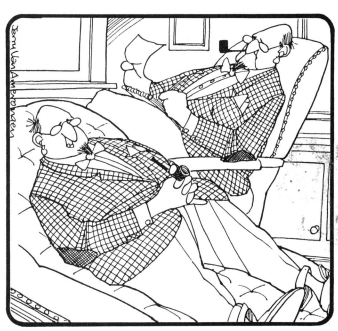

Jason's been in therapy for six years now.

Gil unnerves complete strangers by first photographing them, then hole-punching and wearing their picture around his neck.

Brian is in the shelving and storage business.

Allen creates a stir at the convenience store.

Mrs. Harkey strains the limits of animal dignity.

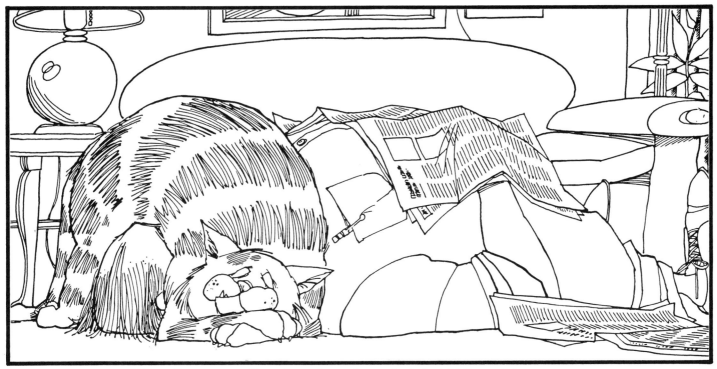

What Stewart at first thought to be a dark forbidding night was actually his cat Harvey.

Howie and the Hog Futures

Aaron applies too much pressure to the toothpaste.

So much for getting "one more year out of the old stand."

Leon enters the "Dress socks as a nuisance factor" essay contest.

Donald feels thoroughly integrated this morning.

Not being a keen observer of corporate
signals, Mr. Curby was shocked when he
was let go.

In a wellness-conscious world, Jason is
glad to be home.

Marian's need to dodge responsibility
caused the lambs to argue with each other
over who dropped the roast.

Surveyor Bud Townsend uses
discarded plumb bobs as articles
of personal adornment.

Boyd Drexler has small motors attached to nearly everything he owns.

Neither of the Simmons brothers can understand why folks are always saying they're bored.

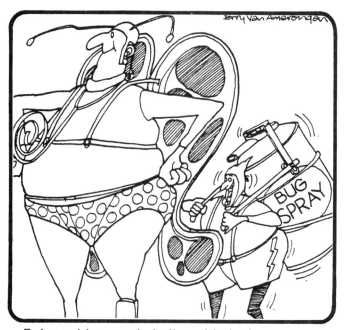

Bob could scarcely believe his luck.

Well, what'll I do... just sniff around or what?...

Bob shows the bookseller that, yes, it is possible to get the book in soft-cover.

Jim stayed in the warming house way too long.

Not surprisingly, Eugene won the car in a drawing.

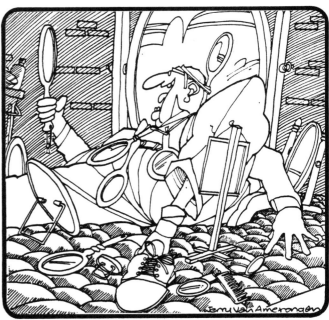

Lyle's long slide began with a piece of reflective metal on the back of his grandfather's pocketwatch.

The Friskys always do little mince steps before dining.

Human anchor Lee Sounder and his friend Emmett

Norris views life from a very short leash.

Allen is dreaming about a gang of bicyclists who, given great powers by their tight little black pants, take control of every city street.

Eugene lacks fiscal responsibility.

After retrieving the paper, Biffy the lap dog is tied up with additional duties.

Cynthia knew it was time to leave when Bruce began slow dancing with a ball.

Another day of uncertainty on Wall Street

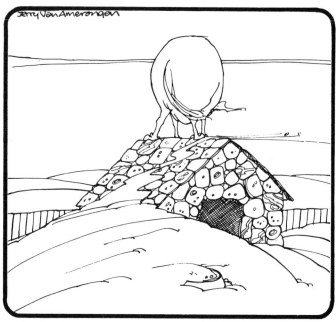

A doghouse made entirely of lunch meat near Fridley, Minn.

Gloria likes to kiss her dog Belcamp until the hair between his ears gets all matted down.

Kevin displays with pride the product of a self-serving crafts class.

Because of Murry's Trailer City location, customers generally visit the kitchen areas first.

While Eugene's competitor was away from the room, a fire broke out in his attache case.

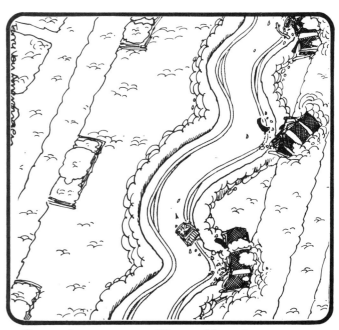

Snowplow operator Digger Mars loses his rhythm.

Monkey see, monkey do.

Samuel has yet to rid his body of its inefficient ways of movement.

Recently, Bob's begun to wonder if it's possible for people to return as pieces of furniture.

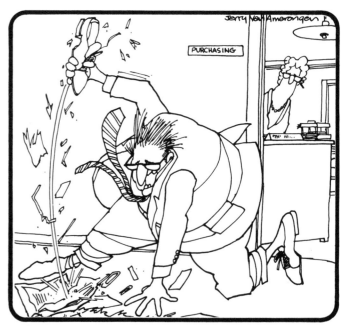

Another salesman begins to emotionally process his distinction as highest bidder.

Ellen's slip is riding up on her again.

It's one of the few tactile pleasures
Grayson allows himself.

Things to do in a closet (Idea No. 5)

Raymond creates a manly climate.

"Oh, oh. Dr. Binghoffer isn't going to be much help today!"

Fly-tying enthusiast Terry Bigalow likes to stress the utilitarian aspects of pet ownership.

When he sold them the house last winter, the Fryhoppers' real estate agent never mentioned that the man next door had an affinity for major appliances.

The tinkling of china and silverware brings mounting tension to the dinner table.

Glenn produces a second form of ID.

Oh, oh, Frank's got hat hair.

Mrs. Gelpy reminds her faithful family friend it's not nice to bark.

WAIT HERE

Elliot generally bends metal tubing that's less than 1 inch in diameter.

Bobby Powers likes to decorate his nose.

Introductions by Roger the tap-dancing dog

During a Zen-like moment, Faber decided to venture out and redirect
his life in accordance with the first sign he came upon.

Mr. Raymond was entirely unprepared for the adjustability of his easy-back adjustable chair.

Gregory introduces his pet to hard candy.

Cynthia continues to be nagged by her husband's insomnia.

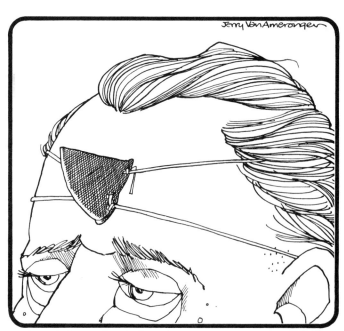

Jacob is a shark fancier.

Why dogs don't wear boxer shorts

Clarence picks the wrong line again.

Allen maximizes his dining experience.

"There it is again," worried Howard, "that sharp pain in the back of my head when I reach down to get the paper."

Apparently Andre still feels the tip belongs to him.

Stanley looked askance at Beverly's easy
Western manner and gay chatter.

Because he ran only the last half-mile of the 10-K race just to get an event T-shirt, the Running Gods made Brian's feet flat.

Sparky joins in the creative process.

Punter Allen Kimberly whips up a batch of scrambled eggs.

Shortly after work begins, Roger disciplines his hammer.

. . . and then Bob blessed all the porch furniture on the block.

Sales manager Harry Kinner makes a cautionary note concerning the new "Full Line at a Glance" presentation case.

Joseph stumbles across his brain's pleasure center.

Years of psychotherapy have so cleared Trudie of excess baggage that she now travels light.

There goes one of the senior people now.

Another muscle-pull means another empty belly for Paul the parrot.

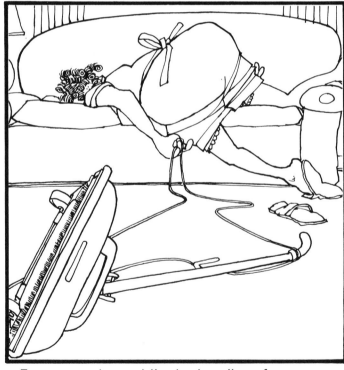

Every once in a while the handles of responsibility feel slippery to Helen.

During the late 1800s, loggers vied for "Best Print Dress on the River" as judged by captured forest creatures.

Salesman Rudy Larson gets another one of those annoying, midmorning, poolside calls from his regional manager.

Stunned by technology

Carlton soon perceives himself to be an open channel of creative energy.

Oftentimes a company's overall personality reflects the style of its top manager.

Suddenly, and without warning, Muriel displays imprinting from a very old part of her brain.

A TV network programmer prepares for another day at the office.

The first thought of many at the table was, "Why did Uncle Carl have BB's in his nose in the first place."

Chef Darnell pauses to gather strength before the diner's shrine, prior to the start of his shift.

Bob's mind is less like a powerful mini-computer and more like a moderately priced blender.

Chad Billingsly experiences a period of disinclination.

Bridget just had a consensus of thought.

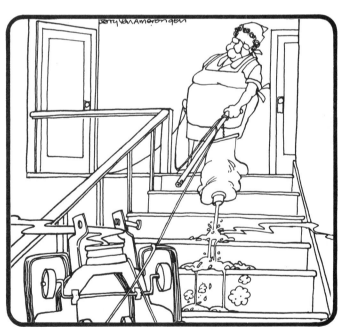

For Peggy this is just another clothespin in the long washline of life.

Suddenly a perfectly good conversation goes haywire.

William's need for attention takes him even higher up the embankment running along the footpath of life.

Suddenly Ravenbrooke lost control of his face.

A worried Marshall Bridges performs a Heimlich maneuver on a pigeon he suspects is choking.

By wearing his cap, Elliot introduces an element of disharmony to the meeting.

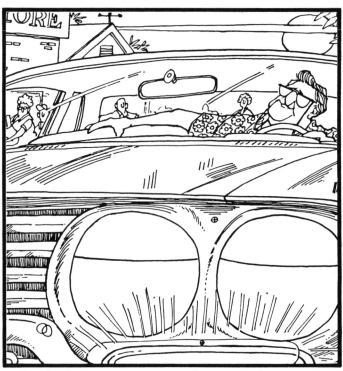

Gordon's present ego needs are such that he spends weekends driving through small towns with his hazard lights on.

Professor Emery and his pet mouse, Larry, perform simple chemistry demonstrations at local shopping centers.

Boyd is a taxidermist with a strong interest in little lap dogs.

Angela has a body image problem.

The aliens have begun their invasion by disguising themselves as service personnel.

Our waiter was refreshingly candid about the caramel custard delight as a dessert choice.

The plane will be in the air another four and a half hours.

YOUR HOROSCOPE

You have a good grip on yourself and your life today.

So much for horoscopes . . .

You can bet the folks down at Smitty's Shady-Time Leisure World are gonna hear about this one.

Georgio Santini does extemporaneous dance in abandoned commercial properties.

Making a pass in the produce section is fraught with risk.

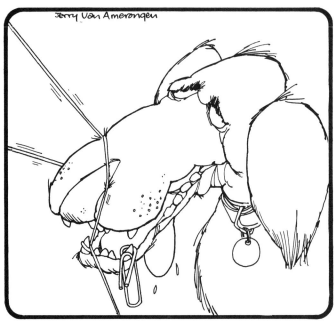

Skipper's interest in office supplies wanes.

Bennett feels good about conversation when he feels good about his support materials.

Another breaching at 2108 Sycamore Lane

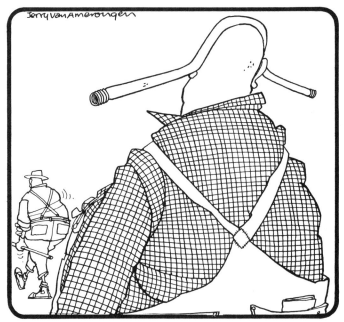

Pipe fitter Benny Selby is fitted by a fellow fitter.

So, thought Andre, still too much pomade.

A retired circus performer trims the lawn.

Everyone on both sides of the relation gets a gift next Christmas.

Sandra begins to spend her many evenings at home with an end table named Larry.

Bobby Tanner proves to be the weak link.

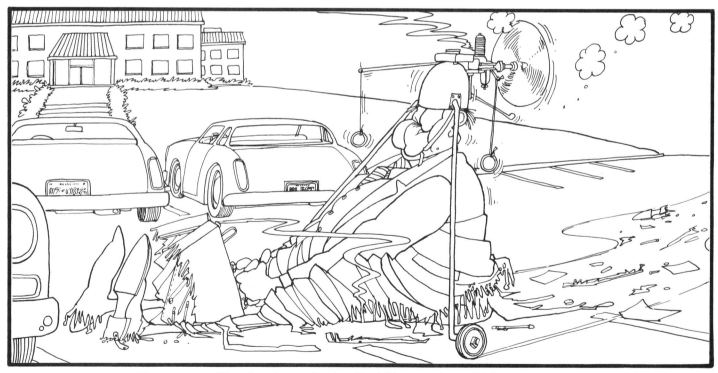

There are still a few bugs in the Earl Hauser Low-Rider.

Human beings appear to be the only creatures who continually check in on their mental status.

Businessman Ed Shippy spends a reflective moment at home before his "Wall of Valor."

Redundancy Beach, California

Darlene's comments about "dry skin" gnawed at Carl all the way home.

Meanwhile, down in the lobby, salesman Biff Simmons wants the contract so badly he can taste it.

Reaction by the sales force to the new price increase wasn't what management had hoped for.

Nelson has allowed for so much leeway in his life, he's beginning to rattle around in it.

Bob can hardly wait for spring.

Bob puts a stop to Mel's argumentative tone.

Norm Sears and Digby Felton are business consultants to privately
owned used-car dealerships of 25 vehicles or less.

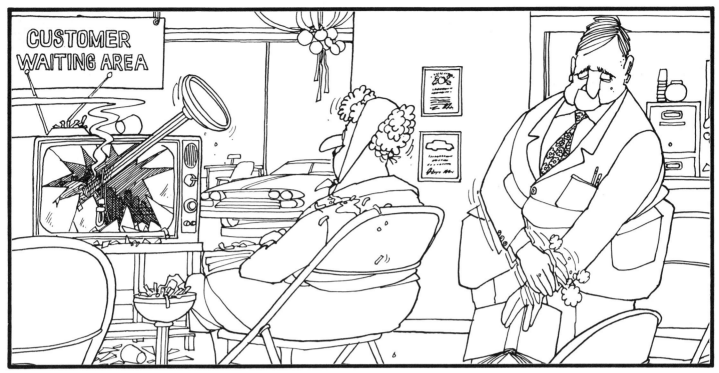

Richard creates a more conducive ambiance for reading.

In an attempt to "touch the face" of humility, attorney Berry Sturpis spends 15 minutes a day in a cheap buffalo suit.

Graham bids goodbye to his low profile.

A dog enjoying a piece of chewing gum

General Manager Smythe hadn't seen his big right-hander swing with that much authority all year.

Jogger Shane Bigalow's had a couple of close calls lately.

All dressed up and no place to go

Harold glimpses the first hint of trouble.

While at the theatre, Jonathan takes the opportunity to alter his consciousness.

Herbert feigns surprise to learn of the aggressive nature of the hamster he managed to unload on his brother-in-law.

Beverly surrenders to the dessert cart.

Norm is confused by simple directions.

". . . and now if you'd step over here, Edgar would like to properly welcome you."

Well, maybe not all . . .

Skeeter was the first of the Saturday afternoon regulars to realize that the little Texan in the corner had a lasso.

Trouble in paradise

Another problem with cheap suits

REX THE WONDER DOG

Biffy's a real pathetic loser.

Certain sound frequencies make Barry Harding do involuntary acts.

The Rhythm-Aires, a precision toothpicking team from Schenectady, New York

You probably wouldn't be surprised to learn that, as children, Phillip and Cornell's parents tried to discourage their friendship.

Sal gets disconnected.

Gregory's interest in the rising water table extends well into the evening hours.

Late last night, Byron was reminded his brother-in-law hadn't returned for the cats.

Even Samuel recognizes he's got a long way to go on the sax.

It looks like Ben's walking in his sleep again.

As it turned out, Bob's new compass provided no real direction.

Muriel and Howard think their dog Marcus across the room to meet the new neighbors.

Eddie's spending way too much time with his pet mouse.

That's it for yo-yoing today.

"I see what you mean," said Mr. Baxter curtly.

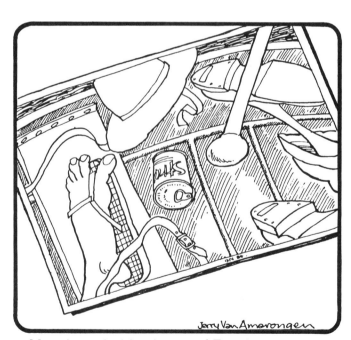

Maggie took this picture of Tom just as he was telling her not to stand up in the canoe.

Russell's quest for uniqueness fades.

Every evening after dinner, Sean Dexter howls three times just like a dog.

Preston, a man with a herd instinct, can never find the herd.

As a means of buying time, Sparky pretends to do some serious sniffing until he can ascertain the mood of his owner.

Bob's as exciting as a protracted discussion about pre-Thanksgiving Day sales.

The Gibsons slept fitfully that night.

What must they think?

Jason retreats to his own personal inner sanctuary.

Occasionally your dog needs to know who the dominant member of the pack is.

Cynthia doesn't like her ankles.

Sparky's due for a nail clip.

Elizabeth loves her new coffee service.

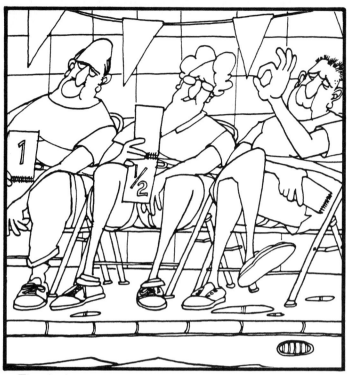

The judges remain unimpressed.

Claudia's nickname is "Footsteps."

A rush of blood to the brain just prior to bridge club is Mrs. Halsey's secret to success.

Now here was a psychologist more suited to Marcia's needs.